Feminism and
the Marxist Movement

Mary-Alice Waters

HOW WINNING THE LIBERATION OF WOMEN IS INSEPARABLY
LINKED TO THE STRUGGLE OF THE WORKING CLASS TO
TRANSFORM ALL ECONOMIC AND SOCIAL RELATIONS

PATHFINDER

NEW YORK   LONDON   MONTREAL   SYDNEY

Mary-Alice Waters is the editor of *New International*, a journal of Marxist politics and theory. Books she has either authored or edited include *Episodes of the Cuban Revolutionary War, 1956–58*; *Che Guevara and the Fight for Socialism Today*; *Communist Continuity and the Fight for Women's Liberation*; *To Speak the Truth: Why Washington's 'Cold War' against Cuba Doesn't End*; *How Far We Slaves Have Come! South Africa and Cuba in Today's World*; *Cosmetics, Fashions, and the Exploitation of Women* (with Joseph Hansen and Evelyn Reed); *Women and the Socialist Revolution*; and *Rosa Luxemburg Speaks*.

COVER DESIGN: *Eva Braiman*

ISBN 978-0-87348-241-7
Library of Congress Control Number 2009930909

Manufactured in Canada

First edition, 1972
Twentieth printing, 2019

PATHFINDER
www.pathfinderpress.com
E-mail: pathfinder@pathfinderpress.com

Feminism and the Marxist Movement

BY MARY-ALICE WATERS

IN HER BOOK, *Woman's Estate,* Juliet Mitchell, the British women's liberation activist and author, puts forward the thesis that "If socialism is to regain its status as *the* revolutionary politics . . . it has to make good its practical sins of commission against women and its huge sin of omission— the absence of an adequate place for them in its theory."

In this she is echoing an opinion that is far from original. Everyone who is active in the women's liberation struggle or familiar with the literature of the movement has heard the same arguments in one form or another. Often we hear the charges: "The Marxist movement has always ignored the problem of women's liberation." "The socialist movement played no significant role in the struggle for women's suffrage, which proves you don't really care about women." Or, "Historically, Marxism hasn't recognized the oppression of women as a sex. It is only concerned with the oppres-

This article was first published in the October 1972 *International Socialist Review.* It is based on a speech given at the Socialist Activists and Educational Conference held in Oberlin, Ohio, August 13–20, 1972.

sion of women as workers."

We have heard such charges repeated so often, either from ignorance or ill will, that sometimes, even unconsciously, we begin to accept the fraudulent version of Marxism and the history of women's struggles that has been concocted to buttress such assertions. The purpose of this talk is to begin to cut through the lies in order to restore the true history of Marxism and women's liberation.

As the new stage of the struggle for women's liberation began to unfold in the late 1960s, the Marxist movement in this country—the Socialist Workers Party (SWP) and the Young Socialist Alliance (YSA)—responded in a revolutionary fashion. We recognized the profound importance of the fact that women as women were beginning to move into action. We threw ourselves into the movement, to learn from it, to better understand it, to help lead it in an independent and fighting direction, and win the most conscious feminists to an understanding that only a socialist revolution could provide the necessary material foundations for the complete liberation of women.

At the same time, we began the process of arming ourselves theoretically. We studied the relevant Marxist classics more deeply than before and tried to apply them to the current reality. We grounded our practice and political orientation in the fundamentals of Marxism.

Now, in addition to action and theory there is a third step we must take. That is to go back and retrace the true lines of our history in order to establish the *continuity* of Marxist theory and practice.

We have a doubly difficult job, however. Not only do we have to contend with the now familiar problems of discovering the true history of women and of writing ourselves as women back into the historical record. We must also cut through the problems created by the fact that most authors who are concerned with women's history are anti-Marxist. They are not interested in discovering what role socialist women played or accurately portraying the political positions taken by revolutionary Marxists. That is a job only we can do.

Is our theory adequate?

I want to begin by stating what I consider to be the most important generalization we must draw from the record of revolutionary Marxism in relation to the struggle against the oppression of women. It is this: From the inception of the Marxist movement to today, for nearly 125 years, revolutionary Marxists have waged an unremitting struggle within the broad working-class movement in order to establish a revolutionary attitude toward the struggle for women's liberation. They have fought to place it on a sound historical and materialist basis; and to educate the entire vanguard of the working class to an understanding of the significance of the struggles by women for full equality and for liberation from the centuries-old degradation of domestic slavery.

This battle has always been one of the dividing lines between revolutionary and reformist currents within the working-class movement; between those committed to a class-struggle perspective and those following a line of class collaboration. Women's oppression and how to struggle against it has been an issue at every turning point in the history of the revolutionary movement. Our ideological and political forebears, the revolutionary Marxists, both male and female, have led the fight against all those who refused to inscribe women's liberation on the banner of socialism, or who supported it in words but refused to fight for it in practice.

This is very important. Our opponents often try to saddle us with responsibility for the positions taken, not by the revolutionaries within the working-class movement, but by the reformists—by the right wing of the pre–World War I American Socialist Party, by the Stalinists, or else by the sectarians and ultralefts who refused to recognize the complexity of the class struggle or the need to fight for democratic rights. But those tendencies do not represent *our* tradition. It is precisely against such forces that revolutionary Marxists have battled over the decades.

The first dividing line came as early as the founding of the Marxist movement itself. The *Communist Manifesto* in 1848 boldly proclaimed:

"On what foundation is the present family, the bourgeois family, based? On capital, on private gain. . . . The bourgeois sees in his wife a mere instrument of production. He hears that the instruments of production are to be exploited in common, and, naturally, can come to no other conclusion than that the lot of being common to all will likewise fall to the women.

"He has not even a suspicion that the real point aimed at is to do away with the status of women as mere instruments of production."

The line of division established here and in all the subsequent writings of Marx and Engels on this subject was that between utopian and scientific socialism. The pre-Marxian utopian socialists—such as Fourier and Owen—were also fervent champions of the emancipation of women. But their socialism, as well as their theories on the family and women, rested on moral principles and abstract desires—not on an understanding of the laws of history and the class struggle rooted in the growth of humanity's productive capacities. Marxism for the first time provided a scientific materialist foundation, not only for socialism but also for women's liberation. It laid bare the roots of women's oppression, its relationship to a system of production based on private property and a society divided between a class that owned the wealth and a class that produced it. Marxism explained the *role* of the family within class society, and the *function* of the family in perpetuating the oppression of women.

More than that, Marxism pointed out the road to achieving women's liberation. It explained how the abolition of private property would provide a material basis for transferring to society as a whole all those onerous social responsibilities today borne by the individual family—the care of the old and sick; the feeding, clothing, and educating of the young. Relieved of these burdens, Marx pointed out, the masses of women would be able to break the bonds of domestic servitude, they would be able to exercise their full capacities as creative and productive—not just reproductive—members of society. Freed from the economic compulsion on which it necessarily rests, the bourgeois family would disappear. Human relationships themselves would be transformed into free relations of free people.

And finally, Marxism took socialism and women's liberation out of the sphere of utopian yearning by proving that capitalism itself produces a force—the working class—strong enough to destroy it, capable of carrying through the momentous task of abolishing the tyranny of the possessing few over the overwhelming majority of humankind. For the first time, socialists could stop wishing for the new and better society and begin to organize to bring it about.

The struggle for women's liberation was thus lifted out of the realm of the personal, the "impossible dream," and unbreakably linked to the victory of the progressive forces of our epoch. It became a social task in the interests of all humanity. Thus, Marxism provided a materialist analysis and a scientific perspective for women's liberation.

Those women like Juliet Mitchell who charge that Marxism does not have an adequate place in its theory for women are being dishonest. It is not the degree of adequacy in Marxism's theory that they really question. They fundamentally disagree with its materialist analysis of women's oppression and all that flows from it, including the need for a revolutionary Marxist party to lead the working class and its allies to power.

Record of the First and Second Internationals

When the First International was founded by Marx and Engels in 1864, socialist theory was put into large-scale organizational practice for the first time. In a radical departure from the laws and customs of the time, the International Working*men's* Association elected a British *woman* trade union organizer, Henrietta Law, to its General Council. How far in advance this step was from the practice of other political organizations of the day can be judged from the fact that Marx tells of receiving letters asking if women would even be allowed to join the International. Marx himself made a motion in the General Council that special working women's branches be organized in factories, industries, and cities where there were large concentrations of women workers, adding that this should in no way cut across the building of mixed branches as well.

A year after the founding of the First International a fight erupted within the German socialist movement between the Marxists and non-Marxists. In the decades ahead the German working class would create the largest, strongest, and most influential socialist party in the pre–World War I era. But from 1865 until well into the 1880s the movement was divided between the followers of the late Ferdinand Lassalle on one hand and the Marxists under the leadership of Wilhelm Liebknecht and August Bebel on the other. In 1875 the two groups united in a single party, the SPD (Sozialdemokratische Partei Deutschlands—Social Democratic Party of Germany), but maintained sharp differences within the organization. A perspective for women's liberation was one question that divided them. The Lassalleans were opposed to demanding equal rights for women as part of the party's program. They believed that women were inferior creatures whose preordained place was in the home and that the victory of socialism would return them to their natural habitat by assuring the husband an adequate wage to provide for his entire family. Thus women would not be forced to work for a wage.

The early programs of the German Social Democrats demanded only "full political rights for adults"—leaving purposely ambiguous the question of whether or not women were considered adults. It was not until the class-struggle left wing succeeded in passing a basically Marxist program in 1891 that the party demanded political rights for all, regardless of sex, and the abolition of every law which discriminated against women in any way.

A decisive element in the victory of the Marxists on this question was the book by August Bebel entitled *Woman and Socialism,* published in 1883. Although it came out a year before Engels's *Origin of the Family, Private Property and the State,* it is basically a development of the ideas outlined by Engels, a powerful explanation of the roots of women's oppression, the forms it has taken over the centuries, the historically progressive effect of the integration of women into industrial production, and the need for a socialist revolution to clear the way for women's liberation. *Woman and Socialism* created a sensation not only in Germany but throughout Europe and was instrumental in the education of several generations of Marxists.

The adoption of a Marxist program, however, was not the end of the struggle within the SPD for a revolutionary position on women's oppression. After the Lassalleans had ceased to exist as a distinct tendency, a new reformist current arose in the party pressing for adaptation to the capitalist status quo on a variety of fronts. Clara Zetkin, one of the staunchest supporters of the Marxist left wing, led the socialist women's movement throughout the entire prewar period and fought within the SPD to develop a revolutionary perspective on the struggle for women's emancipation. Nor was Zetkin's leadership limited to this one question. In 1914, when the majority of the SPD leaders capitulated to German imperialism and voted to support their "own" ruling class in the First World War, Clara Zetkin was one of the tiny handful of German Social Democrats along with Rosa Luxemburg and Karl Liebknecht, who broke with the SPD and maintained a revolutionary internationalist position.

Throughout the early 1890s the SPD concentrated primarily on the trade-union organization of women and made some important gains. Then, in 1896, under Zetkin's urging, the SPD adopted a motion to begin developing special organizations for more extensive political activity among women.

In addition to working for the general aims of the party, they were to concentrate on a whole range of issues of special concern to women: political equality, insurance for childbirth, protective legislation for women workers, education and security for children, and political education for women. Until 1908 it was illegal for women in most of Germany even to join a political group of any kind. The SPD got around this by setting up dozens of "societies for the self-education of women workers," loose associations which were partly outside the boundaries of the party but closely linked to it. From 1900 on, biannual Socialist Women's conferences were held to unite these groups and provide leadership for them.

But the reason for these special working women's organizations was not just to solve the legal problem. Revolutionary leaders of the women's movement in Germany argued for the need to have separate women's organizations on the basis of the special needs of women, their isolation within the family, their fear of speaking out with men around, and the need to develop the leadership capacities of women.

After 1908, women were legally able to join the SPD directly and those in the special SPD women's organizations did. But the women continued to maintain their own newspaper, *Gleichheit* (Equality), edited by Clara Zetkin, which reached a circulation of more than 100,000 by 1912.

They also functioned in a somewhat special way within the SPD. For example, after 1908 women received proportional representation on all the standing committees of the party, and the women members of the committees were elected by meetings of the women comrades. This is interesting, not as a final organizational model, but as an attempt by the SPD to work out difficult problems posed by the need for both independent women's organizations and a single revolutionary party of the working class within which there are no second-class citizens and all members have equal rights and responsibilities.

With sixty or seventy additional years of revolutionary experience behind us, and the examples of the Second and Third Internationals to draw on, revolutionary Marxists have worked out different, and better, solutions to these same problems. There is no separate women's section or caucus within the SWP or YSA. Everyone has equal voice and vote in reaching all decisions on all questions. At the same time, we have special subgroups—we call them "fractions"—to organize and carry out the decisions once they are made and to help lead and direct the work. The Bolsheviks, who had to solve the same problem, likewise drew on these experiences of the German Social Democrats before them and developed an organizational form on which ours is basically modeled.

We should take note of two important points here. First is the realization that questions such as the relationship between a revolutionary party and an independent women's movement and how the leadership of this work within the party should be organized are not new problems that suddenly emerged in 1970. The Marxist movement does have a history and tradition on these questions that is worth studying and learning from.

Second is a word of warning. When we start to look into a historical question like the oppression of women and the struggle against it, we need to guard against the gravest error of all—one that most of our critics in the women's liberation movement make. That is the error of approaching

ROSE PASTOR STOKES

MOTHER JONES

history in an ahistorical way. We must resist the inclination to project backward in time our current level of consciousness or stage of development instead of judging the past by what was known and what was possible then. Unless we take pains at each step to place things in their concrete historical context and understand them in that light, we will not be able to learn from the past.

I want to give three more historical examples of the way in which the question of women's liberation has been an integral part of the struggle to build a revolutionary party of the working class: first, from the early years of the American Socialist Party; second, from the early years of the Third International; and lastly, from the founding of the Fourth International.

The American Socialist Party

The backward, reactionary, patriarchal ideas concerning women's nature which were prevalent in late nineteenth-century society found their reflections within the American socialist movement, just as they did in Germany. That is to be expected. No organization is immune to pressures from the society that surrounds it. But it was the right wing of the socialist movement that acted as the main conduit for sexist ideas. Many in the left wing of the movement fought to establish a correct line in theory and in practice.

For example, it was Daniel DeLeon, the central leader of the Socialist Labor Party and one of the founders of the IWW, the Industrial Workers of the World, who translated Bebel's work, *Woman and Socialism,* for the American public. It was published in this country for the first time in 1904.

Within the Socialist Party, which was founded in 1901, quite discernible right, center, and left wings rapidly materialized. Typical of the attitude held by right-wing elements within the party was an article printed in the April 28, 1901, issue of *The Worker,* one of the many newspapers published unofficially by SP members (the SP had no official press; all its publications were individually owned and controlled and reflected differing points of view). *The Worker* explained that capitalism was forcing women to work because men earned so little. While socialists had no intention of trying to restrict women to the home, once the economic compulsion to work was removed, it was clear that "ninety-nine women out of every hundred would choose the lot of wife and mother."

A widespread attitude within the Socialist Party was similar to the then prevalent view of the Black struggle: women's oppression, like racial oppression, would be solved in passing by the class struggle. It was not a special struggle that had its own dynamic or needed its own organizational forms or put forward its own demands.

James P. Cannon, in his study, *The First Ten Years of American Communism,* describes the left wing of the Socialist Party as a "theoretically uncertain and somewhat heterogeneous minority." It took the Bolshevik revolution and the influence of the ideas and example of Lenin, Trotsky, and the new Third (Communist) International to place this left wing on solid foundations. The young Communist Party of the 1920s brought the American socialist movement out of what Cannon calls the "theoretical wasteland of its prehistory." Cannon explains at length how this help from the Comintern was decisive in educating the young Communist Party on the importance and character of the Black struggle, of convincing the party that Blacks were exploited as Blacks in addition to being exploited as workers, that a program of special demands for this oppressed nationality was needed.

I am sure a similar process took place on the question of women's oppression, as the resolutions of the early years of the Comintern on the organization of work directed specifically to women were far superior to anything the prewar Socialist Party had ever adopted.

However, the question was handled differently than the Black struggle. In the first place, there were several thousand women members of the Socialist Party as compared to a small handful of Black members. And second, the prewar and immediate postwar years saw a massive upsurge in the suffrage struggle, an actual movement involving tens of thousands of women in actions all over the country. These two features produced a real debate within the Socialist Party, and an articulate group of women and men who made their views known and tried to win the Socialist Party to a revolutionary position on feminism, on the importance of the suffrage struggle, and on other demands being raised by women.

I will return a little later to the question of the suffrage struggle, but here I want to give one example of this debate and the views put forward by some of the left-wing members of the American SP.

The *New Review,* a monthly magazine published by SP members, was one of the organs expressing the opinions of the left wing. It frequently carried articles dealing with socialism and feminism. One of the most interesting exchanges occurred in 1914, starting with the March issue. Mary White Ovington (who was also one of the founders of the NAACP) published an article entitled "Socialism and the Feminist Movement." She began by stating that "Socialism and Feminism are the two greatest movements of to-day. The one aims to abolish poverty, the other to destroy servitude among women."

She went on to explain why women were not willing to wait for socialism to begin to struggle for their rights, any more than men were; why this was a revolutionary struggle; and why the Socialist Party should pay more attention to it.

Ovington's defense of the feminist movement elicited a reply, in the May issue of the *New Review,* from British "socialist" E. Belfort Bax who informed her how ignorant she was because he, E. Belfort Bax, had conclusively proved in his book, *The Fraud of Feminism,* that things such as masculine despotism and female "slavery" did not exist. On the contrary, the real problem was that of female privilege, of "woman's immunity from punishment for crimes committed against men."

Bax asserted that it was unfortunate a plank in favor of female suffrage had been included in the party's program, but it was not too late to put an end to such foolishness if people would only think rationally. "Given an average intellectual, and, in certain aspects, moral inferiority of woman as against man . . . there is obvious reason for refusing to concede to woman the right to exercise, let us say, administrative and legislative functions such as have hitherto accrued to men."

Bax's bigoted and pompous opinions brought forth an indignant response. For the rest of the year, month after month, the *New Review* carried articles blasting him. In defense of the term "feminism" one author explained:

"No one doubts that women are changing. We need an appropriate word which will register this fact. The term feminism has been foisted upon us. It will do as well as any other word. . . . It means woman's struggle for freedom." In addition to demands for changes in laws and institutions, the author developed the theme that feminism "means a changed psychology, the creation of a new consciousness in women."

Louise W. Kneeland wrote in the August 1914 issue:

"The Socialist who is not a Feminist lacks breadth. The Feminist who is not a Socialist is lacking in strategy. To the narrow-minded Socialist who says: 'Socialism is a working class movement for the freedom of the working class, with woman as woman we have nothing to do,' the far-sighted Feminist will reply: 'The Socialist movement is the only means whereby woman as woman can obtain real freedom. Therefore I must work for it.'"

Another contribution argued that if women won the right to vote one of the things they must do is "repeal the law which, by penalizing the spread of information in regard to the prevention of conception, attempts to enforce upon women the tyranny of accidental and unwelcome pregnancy." The author added:

"There is certainly no kind of freedom where there is no command over one's own body. If a woman may not keep her body for her own uses as long as she wishes . . . she is certainly a slave."

And so it went, article after article explaining socialism and feminism in terms that sound like they could have been written in the 1970s. Reading such contributions, one senses the depth and breadth of the female radicalization at the beginning of the century, and realizes that there were many socialist women who understood the full significance of that radicalization, identified with it, and participated in it. The fact that they were not able to educate the entire socialist movement to the same level of understanding is attributable to three factors: Social prejudices against women were even deeper and more pervasive than today; American socialism was still in its "theoretical prehistory"; and the majority of the members of the Socialist Party were socialist reformers, not revolutionary Marxists.

Before going on to the early years of the Third International, I want to mention one more aspect of our revolutionary heritage in this country: the Industrial Workers of the World. When most of us think about the heroic battles of the Wobblies, their great free speech fights and strike battles, we don't visualize women as well as men. But one of the most dynamic revolutionary figures of the early years of the century, Elizabeth Gurley Flynn, was a Wobbly organizer for some ten years. She helped lead the famous Spokane, Washington, free speech fight—despite the fact that she was visibly pregnant and, according to the customs of the time, should not even have been seen in public. She played a role in the important IWW-led Lawrence textile strike in 1912 and many others. Both the IWW and the Socialist Party helped lead the hard-fought battles to unionize the textile mills and the garment industry which often employed predominantly female, immigrant labor. Socialist Party leaders and labor organizers like Rose Pastor Stokes, Ella Reeve Bloor, and Mother Jones were women who made historic contributions to American labor and socialist history.

Lenin's views on female emancipation

The Third International was built on the shoulders of the victorious Bolshevik revolution. It was founded when a line of blood was being drawn between the new revolutionary international and the old Social Democracy. No quarter was given to those who wavered between the two. It was a life-and-death struggle for the young Soviet Republic, which was fighting the invading armies of fourteen countries, trying to hold power despite the devastation of war and civil war, famine and disease, in the most economically backward country of Europe.

From 1917 through 1923, the Bolsheviks and many others saw that the struggle for state power was on the agenda not only in Russia but in Germany and other European countries as well. In this they were not wrong. But no leadership other than the Bolsheviks proved capable of meeting the challenge and grasping the historical opportunity to bring the insurgent working masses to the conquest of power.

As the first revolutionary wave subsided, many in the young international failed to understand the meaning of the new situation, the need to readjust the tactics and strategy of the international to accord with the new objective situation, the need to adopt a united-front strategy toward the Social Democracy and other working-class parties. They didn't understand that repeated denunciations of the betrayals by Social Democracy would not by themselves convince those workers still loyal to the Second International. It was necessary to expose the reformist leaders in action.

Lenin and Trotsky together led the fight in the Third International against the ultraleft tendencies that sprang up. They recognized that ultraleftist errors could be just as disastrous for a revolutionary party as reformist ones.

It is in this general political context that Lenin's opinions about the proposed work of the International Women's Commission of the Comintern should be seen. Again, this was at a new turning point in the history of the revolutionary Marxist movement. Again, analysis of women's oppression and the struggle against it figured in the divisions. However, unlike some of the earlier debates and differences, this time many of the opponents of revolutionary Marxism were ultraleft, not reformist.

Clara Zetkin's book, *Recollections of Lenin,* contains the fullest presentation of Lenin's views at this stage. Zetkin's account is based on two meetings with Lenin in Moscow in 1920. These were preliminary discussions, part of the process of drafting the resolution on work among women for the Third Congress of the Comintern in 1921.

First, Lenin urged that the document should stress "the unbreakable connection between woman's human and social position and the private ownership of the means of production." To change the age-old conditions that subjugate women within the family, communists should seek to link the women's movement with "the proletarian class struggle and the revolution." (Clara Zetkin's book is not available in English. Her report of these interviews with Lenin is included in the pamphlet *Lenin On the Emancipation of Women* [Moscow: Progress Publishers, 1968].)

Lenin next took up the organizational questions I referred to earlier. "We derive our organizational ideas from our ideological conceptions," he told Zetkin. "We want no separate organizations of communist women! She who is a Communist belongs as a member to the Party, just as he who is a Communist. They have the same rights and duties."

"However," he continued, "we must not shut our eyes to the facts. The Party must have organs—working groups, commissions, committees, sections or whatever else they may be called—with the specific purpose of rousing the broad masses of women. . . ."

Zetkin commented that many party members had been denouncing her for making similar proposals on the basis that such ideas were a return to Social Democratic traditions, and that "since the Communist Parties gave equality to women they should, consequently, carry on work without differentiation among all the working people in general."

"How," Lenin asked Zetkin, "do such guardians of the 'purity of principles' cope with the historical necessities of our revolutionary policy? All their talk collapses in the face of the inexorable necessities."

"Why are there nowhere as many women in the Party as men," he demanded, "not even in Soviet Russia? Why is the number of women in the trade unions so small?" In sharp terms he defended the need to put forward special demands for the benefit of all women, of working women and peasant women, and even women of the propertied classes who also suffer under bourgeois society.

Finally, Lenin was sharply critical of the national sections of the Comintern for not doing as much as they should. "They adopt a passive, wait-and-see attitude when it comes to creating a mass movement of working women under communist leadership." He attributed the weakness of women's work in the International to the persistence of male chauvinist ideas which led to an underestimation of the vital importance of building a mass women's movement. For this reason he thought the resolution for the Third World Congress of the Comintern was especially important. The fact that it was on the agenda would itself give an impetus to the work of the sections.

Zetkin's second discussion with Lenin conveys an even richer idea of how he (and Zetkin) approached the problem of winning the masses of women on a world scale. It underscored the Bolsheviks' lack of sectarianism or ultraleftism. Their discussion makes clearer than most formal resolutions exactly how they carried out their work.

Zetkin proposed that the communist women from various countries should take the initiative in calling and organizing an international congress of women to help promote the tremendous new ferment and radicalization of women of all classes and sections of society in the post–World War I period. She suggested that they contact ". . . the leaders of the organized female workers in each country, the proletarian political women's movement, bourgeois women's organizations of every trend and description, and finally the prominent female physicians, teachers, writers, etc., and to form national nonpartisan preparatory committees."

The conference, she proposed, should take up questions like the right of women to engage in trades and professions, problems of unemployment, equal pay, labor protection for women, social care for mothers, social measures to relieve housewives, and the status of women in marriage, family legislation, and legal rights. The proposal was based on similar conferences of nonparty working women being organized inside the Soviet Union at that time.

She outlined an international campaign to publicize and build such a conference, and also pointed out how it would be necessary for the communist women themselves to work together in a disciplined fashion in order to bring it off. "Needless to say, all this requires as an essential condition that women Communists work in all the committees and at the congress itself as a firm, solid body and that they act together on a lucid and unshakable plan."

Lenin's reaction was one of wholehearted approval. But he questioned whether the Communist fraction at such a congress on an international scale would be strong enough to win the leadership of the delegates, whether the bourgeois and reformist women might not be stronger. Zetkin responded that she thought it was not a great danger because the communist women would have the best program and proposals for action. And even if they did lose, it would be no disaster. Lenin agreed. "Even defeat after a stubborn struggle would be a gain," he commented.

On further reflection, Lenin pointed out that this congress of women "would foment and increase unrest, uncertainty, contradictions and conflicts in the camp of the bourgeoisie and its reformist friends. . . . The congress would add to the division and thereby weaken the forces of the counterrevolution. Every weakening of the enemy is tantamount to a strengthening of our forces."

With Lenin's backing for the proposal, Zetkin set out to convince the sections of the International of its value, but due to the sectarian opposition of the German and Bulgarian parties, the two parties with the largest women's organizations, the whole project fell through.

What will be most striking to participants in the feminist movement today is the degree to which this proposed conference parallels the general way in which the SWP and YSA have approached the need to build a broad, mass-action-oriented campaign around the abortion issue. The reason we are concentrating at this time on one specific demand out of our whole program for women's liberation is because of the objective possibilities and present level of consciousness. But the method and concept is the same—building a broad, united action front on a principled basis.

The Third International

The resolution that was adopted by the Third Congress of the Comintern in June of 1921 dealt with political and organizational aspects of the International's orientation. The "Theses on Propaganda Work Among Women" began with a concise political analysis stressing both the need for a socialist revolution to achieve women's liberation, and the necessity for the Communist parties to win the support of the masses of women if they were to lead the socialist revolution to victory. Neither could be achieved without the other. The resolution pointed out that if the Communists failed in the task of mobilizing the masses of women on the side of the revolution, the reactionary political forces would try to organize women against them.

It stated that there were no special "female" questions. By this they did not mean that there are no issues of special concern to women or special demands around which women could be mobilized—this is clear from the demands enumerated in the resolution. This statement—which appears often in the literature of the period—simply means that there is no question of concern to women that is not also a broader social question, a question of vital interest to the revolutionary movement, for which both male and female communists must fight. It was directed not against the need to raise special demands for women, but just the opposite, to explain to the more backward male and female workers that such demands cannot be dismissed as unimportant "female concerns."

The resolution also condemned bourgeois feminism.

This designation referred to the section of the women's movement that believed liberation could be achieved by reforming the capitalist system. It called on women to reject that orientation. It likewise called on women to break with the Second International and with the centrists who wavered between the Second and Third internationals and join the Comintern to fight for their liberation on a worldwide scale.

The 1921 thesis of the Comintern explained both why there could be no separate organization for women *within* the party; and on the other hand, why there *must* be special organs of the party for work among women. It made it obligatory, indeed almost a condition of membership in the Communist International, that every section must set up a women's commission structure that would function at every level of the party from the central national leadership to the branches or cells. It instructed the parties to assure that at least one comrade be put on full-time paid staff to direct this work on a national level. And it established an International Women's Secretariat to oversee the work and call regular six-month conferences of representatives from all the sections to discuss and coordinate their activity.

Finally, the resolution outlined the general propaganda and agitational tasks and some of the key demands to be raised in all three sectors of the world: in the Soviet Union, in the advanced capitalist countries, and in the Orient (that is, in the colonial countries that were most in ferment at the time). There was no nonsense such as we hear from ultralefts today who argue that women's liberation is of interest only to the relatively privileged women in the advanced nations or a question that concerns only middle-class women.

In conclusion, the resolution discussed the concrete kinds of action that could help mobilize women throughout the world. These included demonstrations and strikes, public conferences involving nonparty women, classes, cadre schools, the sending of party members into factories where large numbers of women were employed, use of the party press, and so forth. The trade unions and women's professional associations were designated as the central arenas of activity.

This resolution was implemented within the International in a very uneven way, with some sections responding well, and others changing their tempo and character of work very little. One would hardly expect anything else, given the different levels of development of its sections. For example, in the United States, the fledgling CP did establish a women's commission in 1921, but I have been unable to discover anything about what it did or did not do.

At the Fourth Congress of the Comintern, held a year and a half later at the end of 1922, the main line of the 1921 resolution was reaffirmed. The congress called attention to the fact that some sections—unspecified—had not implemented the decisions of the last congress, and urged them to rectify the default. Special mention was made of the effective work among women being done by the Chinese comrades, who had organized themselves along the lines indicated at the Third Congress. The Comintern attached great importance to work among the particularly oppressed women of colonial countries. They realized that there was no possibility of transferring power to the working class in an underdeveloped country any more than in an advanced capitalist country without mobilizing women in struggle for their liberation.

Especially pertinent to this question is an article that appeared in the June 1970 issue of the *International Socialist Review* on "Women in the Chinese Revolution." It is an interview with Chen Pi-lan, today a leader of the Chinese section of the Fourth International, who was recruited to the Chinese Communist Party in 1922 after a CP leader came to her girls' boarding school and gave a speech on "Women's Position in Society." She is an outstanding example of the kind of women who were won to the Marxist movement by the correct policies of the Communist International during its revolutionary years. Chen describes how they organized the girls' school, demanding the right to cut their hair, to have coeducation, to hold discussion circles on questions such as freedom to love and freedom of marriage, in addition to participating in strikes, May Day demonstrations, and forming working women's clubs.

What emerges from this sketchy outline of the political orientation and activities of the Third International during its early years is a strikingly clear picture. And I should point out that within the framework of this talk I have not attempted to deal with the developments that were taking place within the Soviet Union itself. To do so would even further strengthen the positive points I have stressed.

The real situation was far from one of indifference or hostility to the special oppression of women. On the contrary, the Comintern recognized the crucial importance of struggles by women around every question ranging from the right to divorce, to equal pay, to abortion, to communal kitchens and laundry services. They made it mandatory that every section of the International develop a program of demands and an orientation toward winning the leadership of mass struggles by working women, and integrated this work into the perspective of the struggle for power.

Was there resistance to this line, and an unevenness in carrying it out? Yes, of course there was. Just as there was unevenness, resistance, and backwardness on every other question on which the Third International built its foundations. But the leadership of the International *led,* they fought to educate the International and establish the correct political line on this key question. And where it was carried out, the correctness of the orientation was proven many times over.

Were the leaders of the International perfect in their own attitudes or understanding? Did they have the consciousness of communist men and women—or were they even as aware as we are today about the depth of the social prejudices against women, and the way these are reflected in language and innumerable socially accepted stereotypes? Of course not. Feminists today reading Lenin, or the proceedings of the Comintern congresses, or any other literature of that period, will find many examples of pleasantries at the expense of women and language which we would never allow in the revolutionary movement today.

Some point to this as "proof" that the socialist movement doesn't understand the oppression of women. This is simply a dishonest subterfuge, an example of the kind of ahistorical thinking I referred to earlier. It fails to see the wood because some of the leaves are worm-eaten. It's an attempt to substitute subjective criteria for an honest evaluation of the political line advocated, adopted, and carried out by the revolutionary Marxist movement in its evolution. Judging on that basis, which is the only one that counts in the long run, we must say that *the Third International in its early years had a more advanced, revolutionary analysis of women's oppression and the road to liberation than any previous organization in world history.*

It also makes us extremely conscious of the depth of the Stalinist counterrevolution and betrayal. On the question of women's liberation—as on the national question, youth, the united front, and others—broad layers of revolutionaries are only now starting to work back to—or up to—positions that were established by the Bolsheviks some fifty years ago. Humanity has paid an incalculable price for the break in the continuity of Marxist traditions during that lost half-century.

The Fourth International

The revolutionary ideas and methods of the early Comintern did not die with the Stalinization of the International and the political counterrevolution in the Soviet Union in the late 1920s. They were carried on by the Soviet Left Opposition, and then by the International Left Opposition. They became the bedrock on which the Trotskyist Fourth International was built. Once again, as with all the earlier turning points in the history of revolutionary Marxism, the question of women's liberation was one of the differences which divided revolutionaries from nonrevolutionaries.

The years of isolation, the economic backwardness of pre–World War I Russia, the terrible devastation of imperialist war and civil war, the great human price paid by the October Revolution in its struggle for survival were too much. The revolution could not emerge unscathed. While capitalism was not restored, under Stalin's leadership the privileged bureaucracy acquired a more and more deadly stranglehold on the revolution in all spheres—foreign policy, national minorities, political freedom, economic planning, education, etc. As an integral part of this process the gains made by women following the October Revolution were reversed, one after the other. The family was replaced on its pedestal, abortions were made illegal, divorce became more and more difficult and costly, prostitution and homosexuality again became crimes punishable by imprisonment, day-care centers were closed or their hours shortened, coeducation was eventually eliminated, and more.

Again and again the Left Opposition led by Trotsky sounded the alarm against these measures and exposed what they meant, both on the ideological plane and on the level of human suffering for millions of women. In *The Revolution Betrayed* Trotsky devoted an entire chapter to the effects of the Stalinist reaction on women and the family. He explained the material reasons why the revolution was unable to provide the necessary alternatives to the family system, and why the privileged bureaucracy was compelled in its own self-interest to reinforce the family and deepen the oppression of women.

In 1938, in an article entitled "Does the Soviet Government Still Follow the Principles Adopted Twenty Years Ago?," Trotsky summarized the process by which the gains made by women after the revolution were reversed:

"The position of *woman* is the most graphic and telling indicator for evaluating a social regime and state policy. The October Revolution inscribed on its banner the emancipation of womankind and created the most progressive legislation in history on marriage and the family. This does not mean, of course, that a 'happy life' was immediately in store for the Soviet woman. Genuine emancipation of women is inconceivable without a general rise of economy and culture, without the destruction of the petty-bourgeois economic family unit, without the introduction of socialized food preparation, and education. Meanwhile, guided by its conservative instinct, the bureaucracy has taken alarm at the 'disintegration' of the family. It began singing panegyrics to the family supper and the family laundry, that is, the household slavery of woman. To cap it all the bureaucracy has restored criminal punishment for abortions, officially returning women to the status of pack animals. In complete contradiction with the ABC of Communism the ruling caste has thus restored the most reactionary and benighted nucleus of the class regime, i.e., the petty-bourgeois family." (*Writings of Leon Trotsky: 1937–38* [New York: Pathfinder Press, 1970, 1976], pp. 166–67 [2016 printing].)

In such terms the positions of revolutionary Marxism were carried over into our heritage upon the founding of the Socialist Workers Party and the Fourth International. We can proudly and legitimately lay claim to the unbroken continuity of a 125-year struggle by the Marxist movement against women's oppression, and to establish a socialist world which alone can lay the basis for the liberation of women. Everything we do and say today is in harmony with this tradition, and a continuation of it.

The suffrage movement and 'bourgeois feminism'

I want now to deal specifically with the suffrage movement because there is probably no other single chapter in the history of women's struggles where the position and role of socialists has been so falsified, misunderstood, or distorted.

The problem is two-sided. On the one hand, the popular historians of the suffrage movement, who are mostly anti-

Marxist, have had little interest in ferreting out the role of the socialist movement. One can read book after book on the suffrage campaign and not come across even a passing reference to the participation of Marxist women.

On the other hand, many sectarian or ultraleft "socialists" have taken the position that the suffrage movement was for nothing but a trivial bourgeois reform, a diversion from the real class struggle, of no concern to working-class women who did not at all benefit from winning such a nebulous democratic right under capitalism. These so-called socialists have had no interest in discussing the real record of the revolutionary parties in the fight for female suffrage either, as it would completely contradict their fanciful sectarian interpretations.

To begin with, let me take up one question that has bothered a good many who have read some of the socialist literature on the suffrage and feminist movement at the turn of the century. Over and over, the articles and resolutions denounce "bourgeois feminism," or just plain feminism, as a threat to the working-class movement. Even today, women in organizations like the International Socialists or other sectarian groups use such references to accuse the Trotskyists of breaking with the Marxist tradition of implacable opposition to bourgeois feminism.

What was the real point at issue? What is bourgeois feminism? And why was so much fire directed against it?

First let's dispose of a misunderstanding which sometimes makes communication difficult even today. It happens that the European radical movement has always used the term feminism as synonymous with opposition to a materialist analysis of women's oppression. In this usage, a feminist is someone who consciously rejects the idea that we must abolish private property if we are to achieve women's liberation. Socialism and feminism are thus mutually exclusive.

The American radical movement—as we saw even from the articles in the *New Review*—has not always used the terms in that way. For us a feminist is any woman who recognizes that women are oppressed as a sex and is willing to carry out an uncompromising struggle to end that oppression. Thus we say the most consistent feminist must be a socialist. This difference in terminology often causes confusion and misunderstandings.

The goal of the nineteenth- and early twentieth-century suffrage movement was to achieve a reform in the voting laws, to further democratize the electoral base in the existing bourgeois states. It was a continuation of the struggle to extend the franchise to the masses that began with the crest of the bourgeois-democratic revolution in the late eighteenth century. In the United States, universal white male suffrage had been achieved by the 1830s or 1840s through a series of struggles and reform laws that finally eliminated property qualifications for white males over twenty-one years old. With the post–Civil War enfranchisement of Black male adults—the formal if not real enfranchisement—only women were denied the vote.

In Europe it was different. In most countries universal male suffrage had not been won, and often the suffrage struggle was a combined one for males and females.

As with all struggles for reforms, the suffrage movement affected and involved many different layers and all classes of society. The reform was not in and of itself unacceptable to the ruling class, the bourgeoisie. Within the limits of parliamentary democracy it could be used as a de-

vice to undercut the deepening working-class radicalization and further disguise the class nature of the capitalist
state. After all, if every adult has one vote, and the poor
obviously outnumber the rich by millions to one, isn't the
government they elect evidently subservient to the interests of the workers?

But the fight for democratic reforms is also in the interests of the working class, as Lenin explained over and over
again. It is what he called the ABC of Marxism. For example, in rejecting the views of one P. Kievsky, who had argued that socialists should abstain from the fight to win for
women the right of divorce on the grounds that such a reform would be meaningless under capitalism, Lenin said:

"That objection reveals complete failure to understand
the relation between democracy *in general* and capitalism.
The conditions that make it impossible for the oppressed
classes to 'exercise' their democratic rights are not the ex-
ception under capitalism; they are typical of the system.
In most cases the right of divorce will remain unrealizable
under capitalism, for the oppressed sex is subjugated economically. No matter how much democracy there is under
capitalism, the woman remains a 'domestic slave', a slave
locked up in the bedroom, nursery, kitchen. . . .

"Only those who cannot think straight or have no knowl-
edge of Marxism will conclude: so there is no point . . . in
freedom of divorce, no point in democracy. . . . But Marxists know that democracy does *not* abolish class oppression. It only makes the class struggle more direct, wider,
more open and pronounced, and that is what we need. The
fuller the freedom of divorce, the clearer will women see
that the source of their 'domestic slavery' is capitalism, not
lack of rights. The more democratic the system of govern-

ment, the clearer will the workers see that the root evil is capitalism, not lack of rights. . . .

"All 'democracy' consists in the proclamation and realization of 'rights' which under capitalism are realizable only to a very small degree and only relatively. But without the proclamation of these rights, without a struggle to introduce them now, immediately, without training the masses in the spirit of this struggle, socialism is *impossible."* (From "A Caricature of Marxism and Imperialist Economism," written August–October 1916. In Lenin's *Collected Works* [Moscow: Progress Publishers, 1964], Vol. 23, pp. 72–74.)

It was in that spirit that revolutionary Marxists fought unconditionally for full male and female suffrage.

It was in the quite different spirit of reforming capitalism in order to improve an already "good system" that many bourgeois and middle-class women participated in the suffrage struggle. And they took positions that reflected their upper-class, anti-working-class bias—to use Marxist terminology, their bourgeois bias. Many women honestly believed that once women gained the vote they could rid capitalism of its wars, poverty, and other evils.

In England, prior to World War I, most of the suffrage movement was demanding the vote for women on "equal terms with men." This meant on the basis of property restrictions that would have disfranchised most working-class women. Revolutionists opposed this, of course. They demanded universal female and male suffrage, nothing less. Such a fundamental difference was a difference in class outlook and program, and thoroughly justified the designation of the half-way suffragists as bourgeois in their political perspective.

In both the United States and Britain, the majority of the suffragists supported their "own" bourgeois government in the first imperialist world war. All revolutionary Marxists—male and female—opposed that war, and a class line was drawn on that question as well.

Many women within the suffrage movement opposed the perspective of independent mass actions by women to win the vote and other forms of militant tactics aimed at involving large numbers of women. For us the strategy of mobilizing the masses to take control of their own destiny is a *class* question, a question of principle.

Many suffragists in the United States appealed to racist and anti-immigrant prejudices. They argued that women should have the vote to save the South from being controlled by Blacks and the North and West by foreigners.

Revolutionary Marxists condemned such positions, fought against them, and refused to be identified with them. That is no different from what we do today. Today we polemicize with "bourgeois" and "petty-bourgeois" feminists who believe that liberation can be achieved or even advanced by voting for McGovern or some other capitalist party candidate. In the same way, we direct our fire against those feminists who oppose the perspective of mobilizing masses of women and believe they can find a personal solution either by individually dropping out of the system or by making it within the system.

In the same way we polemicize with those feminists who believe that class divisions and exploitation stem from sex oppression and not vice versa. In the same way we try to win the largest possible number of fighting women to our banner because we know that only by building a mass revolutionary party can we assure the victory of the socialist revolution and gain women's liberation.

In that sense we agree 100 percent with the condemnation of "bourgeois" feminism and our fight today is simply a continuation of our forebears' fight to win the women's movement to a working-class perspective.

Having said that, it should also be added that some of the nineteenth- and early twentieth-century attacks on bourgeois feminism did not stem from such political or revolutionary considerations. There is no doubt that many reformist, pseudosocialist, and just plain backward but revolutionary-minded men and women often used the term bourgeois feminism not as a scientific political designation, but as an epithet, an easy way to cover up for their chauvinist prejudices against women. This is basically what Lenin was referring to when he told Clara Zetkin, "we must root out the old slave-owner's point of view, both in the Party and among the masses."

If we often avoid terms like "bourgeois" or "petty-bourgeois" feminism today, it is because they are not widely understood. Over the years they have been so misused in the radical movement that they usually obscure differences rather than clarify them.

The question of "bourgeois feminism" also arose in connection with the organizational relationship between the broad suffrage movement and the work done by the socialist parties.

For example, at the world congress of the Second International held in Stuttgart, Germany, in 1907, a resolution on the fight for women's suffrage was passed which said, among other things, that women workers should campaign for the franchise, not in conjunction with the bourgeois supporters of women's rights, but in conjunction with the class parties of the proletariat. In 1908 the convention of the Socialist Party in this country passed a similar resolution. What exactly did this involve? We can be sure that such resolutions were sometimes used as justifications for a sectarian abstention from the suffrage struggle, but that was not the intent of the motions.

Such statements did not mean that the socialists would refuse to collaborate, or cooperate, or work with non-socialists or anyone else. What they did mean was that revolutionaries would refuse to compromise on questions of class principle such as the attitude to imperialist war, racism, etc. They also meant that the Social Democratic parties would carry out a campaign for suffrage in their own name. We should not forget that these were mass parties, with tens of thousands or hundreds of thousands of members, leading the entire trade-union movement in country after country. And when they talked about organizing their own forces to fight, they were talking about mass participation.

If the Socialist Workers Party was strong enough today to mobilize 30,000 or 50,000 women in the streets of New York demanding abortion-law repeal under our own banner, you can be sure we would do it. This would not be a refusal to work with other forces, or to join together to mobilize 100,000 or a million under a united-front formation. But if it were feasible we would not hesitate to call such actions on our own and urge the masses of workers to join with us, not with Shirley Chisholm or Betty Friedan.

What is meant by not collaborating with bourgeois women is well explained by Bebel in his introduction to *Woman and Socialism*. He sharply attacks the idea that women from different classes cannot fight alongside one another for specific demands aimed at eliminating the oppression of *all* women. He points out:

"The class-antagonism, that in the general social movement rages between the capitalist and the working class, and which, with the ripening of conditions, grows sharper and more pronounced, turns up likewise on the surface of the Woman's Movement; and it finds its corresponding expression in the aims and tactics of those engaged in it.

"All the same, the hostile sisters have, to a far greater extent than the male population—split up as the latter is in the class struggle—a number of points of contact, on which they can, although marching separately, strike jointly. This happens on all the fields, on which the question is the equality of woman with man, within modern society." (Published in this country as *Woman Under Socialism* [New York: Schocken Books, 1971], p. 5.)

Bebel's formula, "marching separately, strike jointly," the classic definition of the united-front tactic, was proposed more than forty years before it became the byword of the Third International under Lenin and Trotsky.

Socialists in the suffrage struggle

Let's review the record of what the parties of the Second and Third Internationals actually did to help win the suffrage struggle.

First, and not the least important, was that they established a clear line of principle on what they were fighting for. This was settled at the 1907 Stuttgart Congress of the Second International. The Austrian Social Democrats were then in the midst of a suffrage fight, and they had decided that the key task was winning universal male enfranchisement. Arguing that the demand for women's suffrage might endanger the possibility of winning the vote for working men, Victor Adler and the other reformist Austrian leaders decided not to campaign for female suffrage.

Clara Zetkin and others demanded that this question be settled by the international congress. After debate the congress voted to condemn the Austrian party for sacrificing the principle of equal rights for women to what the Austrians thought would be a more expedient position vis-a-vis the male workers.

The same question came up in Belgium, where the Social Democracy was led—as in Austria—by openly reformist forces. In 1902 and again in 1918 the Social Democrats refused to demand suffrage rights for women because they believed that most women would vote for the reactionary Catholic parties. Belgian women did not win the right to vote until after World War II.

Against this background, the fight to pass a principled, revolutionary position on women's suffrage was not an insignificant question.

With a clear, principled line established, the second important thing the Social Democracy did was make the campaign for women's suffrage international in scope. This was the origin of March 8 as International Women's Day. We know from experience in the antiwar movement that organizing and building internationally coordinated actions is no small job, and we shouldn't underestimate the impact and power of the Second International's campaign on this issue.

Taking their inspiration from the mass actions for women's suffrage organized by the socialist women in the United States, the International Socialist Women's Congress in 1910 called for an international day of action demanding universal female suffrage. The unifying theme was to be:

"The vote for women will unite our strength in the struggle for socialism." The response to the call was beyond all expectations.

In Germany and Austria, for example, the action was broadly built: committees were formed, publicity put out, demonstrations and meetings organized, articles prepared for the press. Special newspapers were issued the week before the day of action. *The Vote for Women* appeared in Germany and *Women's Day* in Austria.

Alexandra Kollontai, the Russian revolutionary women's leader, described the turnout for the first Women's Day in 1911 in the following way:

"Germany and Austria . . . were one seething trembling sea of women. Meetings were organized everywhere—in the small towns and even in the villages. Halls were packed so full that they had to ask workers to give up their places to the women. This was certainly the first show of militancy by the working women. Men stayed at home with the children for a change, and their wives, the captive housewives, went to meetings." (*International Women's Day* by Alexandra Kollontai [London: North London Socialist Woman, 1972], p. 2.)

In Austria, 30,000 women and men took part in the largest street demonstration. Thereafter, International Women's Day became an annual event.

In the United States, too, the Socialist Party played an important role in the final stage of the suffrage struggle, from 1907–08 on. Party conventions discussed and debated how to participate in and organize the suffrage campaign; demonstrations and meetings were organized—demonstrations called by the party itself as well as broader ones in which the socialists took part.

In 1907, the publication *The Socialist Woman* was created as one of the many SP-oriented journals. Wherever the SP had legislators they introduced suffrage bills. In 1909, women's suffrage was one of the themes of the May Day meetings and actions. And in 1908, the party selected a full-time paid organizer to direct the work on a national scale.

In at least three states the Socialist Party campaigns around the suffrage issue played an important and perhaps decisive part in the winning of the franchise: Nevada, Kansas, and the crucial 1917 battle in New York. During the height of the New York fight, the Socialist Party organized suffrage meetings somewhere in the city every single night. SP strength in both upstate New York and New York City was probably decisive in securing the narrow margin of victory.

The Socialist Party also ran many women candidates for office, which was a demonstrative step to take. For example, Kate Richards O'Hare ran for the House in Kansas in 1910, Anna A. Maley for governor of Washington in 1912, and Ella Reeve Bloor for lieutenant governor of New York in 1918.

Far from the suffrage struggle passing the Socialist Party by, as one would assume from numerous accounts, many of the most articulate and skilled women—and certainly the most politically conscious—were in the Socialist Party. The SP was a mass party with tens of thousands of members. Feminists and suffragists like Rheta Childe Dorr joined the Socialist Party when they came to realize, as Dorr explained, that "full equalization of the laws governing men and women are part of the Socialist platform in every country of the world."

A roster of women who were in the Socialist Party reads

like an honor roll of the early decades of the century: Ella Reeve Bloor, Mary Mother Jones, Kate Richards O'Hare, Margaret Sanger, Helen Keller, Anna Louise Strong, Rose Pastor Stokes, Antoinette Konikow, and many more.

In fact, Ida Husted Harper, author of the *History of Woman Suffrage, 1900–1920,* testified before the House Judiciary Committee in 1912 that the Socialist Party was "the only one which declares for woman suffrage and thereby gives women an opportunity to come out and stand by it." In her opinion this explained "why there seem to be more Socialist women than Republican or Democratic." (Cited by James Weinstein in *The Decline of Socialism in America, 1912–1925* [New York: Monthly Review Press, 1967], p. 62.)

The fact that the Socialist Party fought for women's suffrage was one reason why the SP attracted more outspoken women leaders than the capitalist parties. But that was not all that was involved. The decision to join the revolutionary working-class movement represented a qualitatively higher level of consciousness concerning the problems of women's oppression and what would be necessary to achieve liberation. The women who joined the Socialist Party did so because they understood that the only key which could open the door to their liberation as a sex was the transfer of state power from the hands of the capitalist rulers to the working class.

The Bolsheviks and the suffrage movement

The party that made the greatest contribution to the struggle for women's suffrage, however, was not the amorphous American SP but the more unequivocally revolutionary Russian Bolsheviks. And their contribution was not only national but international in scope.

Despite the illegal conditions of czarist repression, both the Mensheviks and the Bolsheviks organized activities for International Women's Day starting in 1913. Alexandra Kollontai describes how they organized an illegal "Morning Teach-In on the Woman Question" in Petrograd in 1913 (at the end of which almost all the party speakers were arrested). She points out what an inspiration this action was— despite the arrests—to others around the world.

Those early actions in 1913 and 1914 laid the basis for the massive women's demonstration of March 8, 1917 (February 23 by the Russian calendar), when the Petrograd women poured into the streets demanding "Bread for our children," and "The return of our husbands from the trenches." The Russian Revolution marked its beginning from that day.

The legal equality won by the women of Soviet Russia was a tremendous embarrassment to the so-called democracies around the world where women were denied the right to vote. Women in Russia won the franchise with the February Revolution and during 1917–18 pickets at the White House frequently carried placards contrasting "Free Russia" with "Kaiser Wilson."

Supporters of the Women's Party in the U. S. started a "watch fire" in an urn in front of the White House and every time Wilson made a speech abroad that referred to freedom, even in passing, a copy of the speech was burned in the watch fire. Women around the world gained powerful support in their suffrage demands from the fact that even in "backward" Russia women had won the right to vote.

With the victory of the Bolsheviks in October, a woman assumed a cabinet post for the first time in history. Alexandra Kollontai became the head of the Social Welfare Ministry. When Kollontai was later appointed the first woman ambassador in history, the aristocratic diplomatic corps of the world was rocked by convulsions. Not only was she a woman, but a "morally loose" one at that, who was hardly fit to associate with kings, queens, and heads of state.

We can point to the victory of the Russian Revolution and the establishment of the first workers' state in the world as an historic contribution by our forebears to the struggle for women's suffrage, women's liberation, and the progress of all humanity.

What I have tried to do in this talk should be seen as a beginning. Much more research needs to be done. As we unearth new material, discover new sources, and establish new facts, new conclusions will inevitably suggest themselves. We may want to modify, adjust, or further develop our initial impressions and evaluations. But this is the beginning of the process of retying the threads of continuity in our Marxist history and renewing our traditions. The deeper we go in this process of rediscovering our own past, the richer will be our understanding of today, the better prepared and more confident we will be to break new ground as we face new tasks and challenges in the future.

ALSO BY MARY-ALICE WATERS

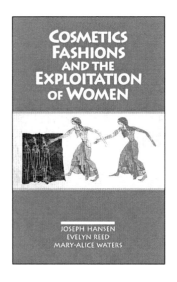

Cosmetics, Fashions, and the Exploitation of Women

JOSEPH HANSEN, EVELYN REED, MARY-ALICE WATERS

How big business plays on women's second-class status and economic insecurities to market cosmetics and rake in profits. And how the entry of millions of women into the workforce has irreversibly changed relations between women and men—for the better. $15. Also in Spanish and Farsi.

Is Socialist Revolution in the US Possible?

A Necessary Debate among Working People

MARY-ALICE WATERS

An unhesitating "Yes"—that's the answer given here. Possible—but not inevitable. That depends on what working people *do*. $10. Also in Spanish, French, and Farsi.

Che Guevara and the Imperialist Reality

Ernesto Che Guevara was among the most outstanding leaders forged by Cuba's socialist revolution. The internationalist course he helped lead strengthened not only the Cuban Revolution but the working class and its allies within the US itself. In a world still dominated by imperialism, Waters notes, the odds have shifted in favor of the oppressed and exploited. $6. Also in Spanish.

THE CLASS STRUGGLE IN THE UNITED STATES

The Clintons' Anti-Working-Class Record
Why Washington Fears Working People

JACK BARNES

Describes the profit-driven course of Democrats and Republicans alike, and the political awakening of workers seeking to understand and resist these assaults. $10. Also in Spanish, French, and Farsi.

Are They Rich Because They're Smart?
Class, Privilege, and Learning under Capitalism

JACK BARNES

Exposes the self-serving rationalizations by well-paid middle-class layers that their intelligence and schooling equip them to "regulate" workers' lives. Includes "Capitalism, the Working Class, and the Transformation of Learning." $10. Also in Spanish, French, and Farsi.

50 Years of Covert Operations in the US
Washington's Political Police and the American Working Class

LARRY SEIGLE, FARRELL DOBBS, STEVE CLARK

How class-conscious workers have fought against the drive to build the "national security" state essential to maintaining capitalist rule. $12. Also in Spanish and Farsi.

WOMEN'S LIBERATION AND SOCIALISM

Women in Cuba: The Making of a Revolution within the Revolution
Vilma Espín, Asela de los Santos, Yolanda Ferrer

The integration of women into the ranks and leadership of the Cuban Revolution was inseparably intertwined with the proletarian course of the revolution from the start. This is the story of that revolution and how it transformed the women and men who made it. $20. Also in Spanish and Greek.

Women's Liberation and the African Freedom Struggle
Thomas Sankara

"There is no true social revolution without the liberation of women," explains the leader of the 1983–87 revolution in the West African country of Burkina Faso. $8. Also in Spanish, French, and Farsi.

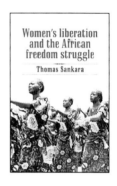

Abortion Is a Woman's Right!
Pat Grogan, Evelyn Reed

Why abortion rights are central not only to the fight for the full emancipation of women, but to forging a united and fighting labor movement. $6. Also in Spanish.

Communist Continuity and the Fight for Women's Liberation
Documents of the Socialist Workers Party, 1971–86

How did the oppression of women begin? Who benefits? What social forces have the power to end women's second-class status? 3 volumes, edited with preface by Mary-Alice Waters. $30

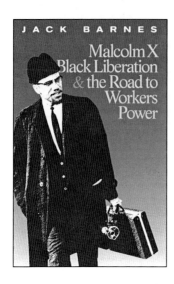

"It's the Poor Who Face the Savagery of the US 'Justice' System"

The Cuban Five Talk about Their Lives within the US Working Class

How US cops, courts, and prisons work as "an enormous machine for grinding people up." Five Cuban revolutionaries framed up and held in US jails for 16 years explain the human devastation of capitalist "justice"—and how socialist Cuba is different. $15. Also in Spanish, Farsi, and Greek.

The History of the Russian Revolution

LEON TROTSKY

How, under Lenin's leadership, the Bolshevik Party led millions of workers and farmers to overthrow the state power of the landlords and capitalists in 1917 and bring to power a government that advanced their class interests at home and worldwide. Unabridged, 3 vols. in one. Written by one of the central leaders of that socialist revolution. $38. Also in French and Russian.

Teamster Rebellion

FARRELL DOBBS

The 1934 strikes that won union recognition for truckers and warehouse workers in Minneapolis and helped pave the way for the working-class social movement that built the industrial unions. The first of four volumes by a central leader of these battles. $19. Also in Spanish, French, Farsi, and Greek.

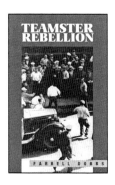